Too many Whites

Alexandria Ocasio-Cortez @AOC · Jun 9

US House candidate, NY-14

Our first slate of New York primary endorsements is out today!

New York: The primary election is on June 23rd.

Early voting starts THIS Saturday, June 13th!

Check ocasiocortez.com/vote to find your early polling location.

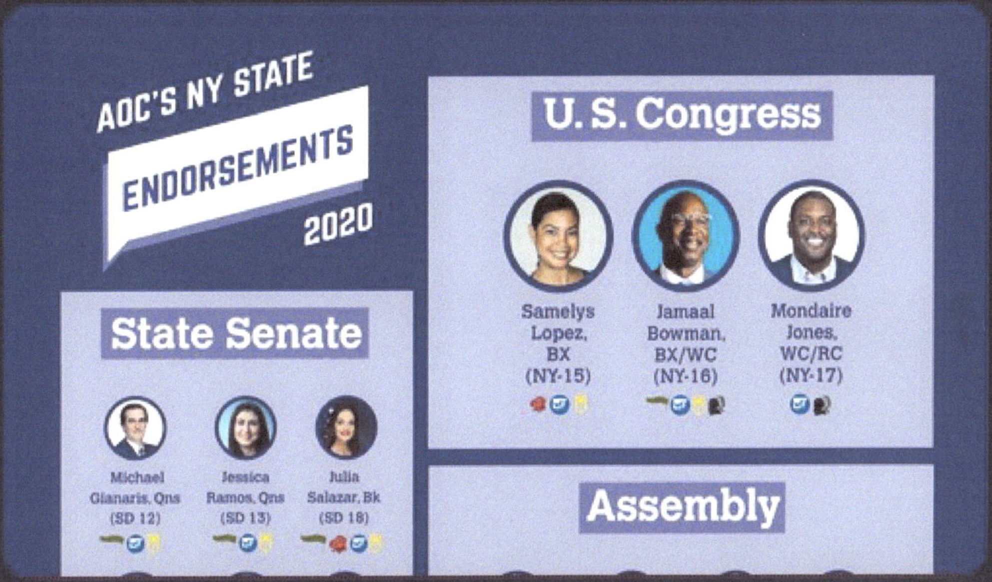

Communist Party of China
@CommunistsChina

Replying to @AOC

Too many white people...

In Communist China, there are no executions without trial. Chairman is strict!

Donald J. Trump @realDonaldTrump · May 20

So true. OBAMAGATE!

> **Ted Cruz** @tedcruz · May 20
>
> Wow. Ongoing spying from an outgoing POTUS on the incoming POTUS—directed by Obama himself—is unprecedented in the 243 years of our nation's history. twitter.com/seanmdav/statu...

Communist Party of China
@CommunistsChina

Replying to @realDonaldTrump

Chairman Mao demands that former FBI director Rod Rosenstein not be executed for treason without trial.

Rosenstein admits Russia collusion was baseless, washes hand...

The Rod Rosenstein Senate hearing was all fireworks as new revelations were spotlighted. One America's Chanel Rion has

youtube.com

Communist Party of China @CommunistsChina

Chairman Mao demands that @realDonaldTrump not execute Rashida Tlaib without proper trial.

House Ethics Committee Finds Rashida Tlaib Violated Campaign Finance Rules

*"...impeach the motherf**ker..."?*

AP - THE DEFINITION OF FAKE NEWS

APStylebook @APStylebook · Sep 30

New guidance on AP Stylebook Online:

Use care in deciding which term best applies:
A riot is a wild or violent disturbance of the peace involving a group of people. The term riot suggests uncontrolled chaos and pandemonium. (1/5)

APStylebook @APStylebook · Sep 30

Focusing on rioting and property destruction rather than underlying grievance has been used in the past to stigmatize broad swaths of people protesting against lynching, police brutality or for racial justice, going back to the urban uprisings of the 1960s. (2/5)

APStylebook @APStylebook · Sep 30

Unrest is a vaguer, milder and less emotional term for a condition of angry discontent and protest verging on revolt. (3/5)

Communist Party of China
@CommunistsChina

Replying to @APStylebook

Chairman make laugh. Say imperialist Americans steal Communist playbook! Chairman say inveterate liars of *Pravda* or *People's Daily* no match for AP style guide writers.

CNN - Very Fake News

Communist Party of China @CommunistsChina · 15h

Are we living in a matrix? Is EVERYTHING FAKE?

- Cover of Brian Stelter's book looks like it was made in MS Paint.
- Its Amazon book store URL has 'Untitled' in it.
- The publisher got a paid-for review (Kirkus).
- The book was heavily promoted on ...

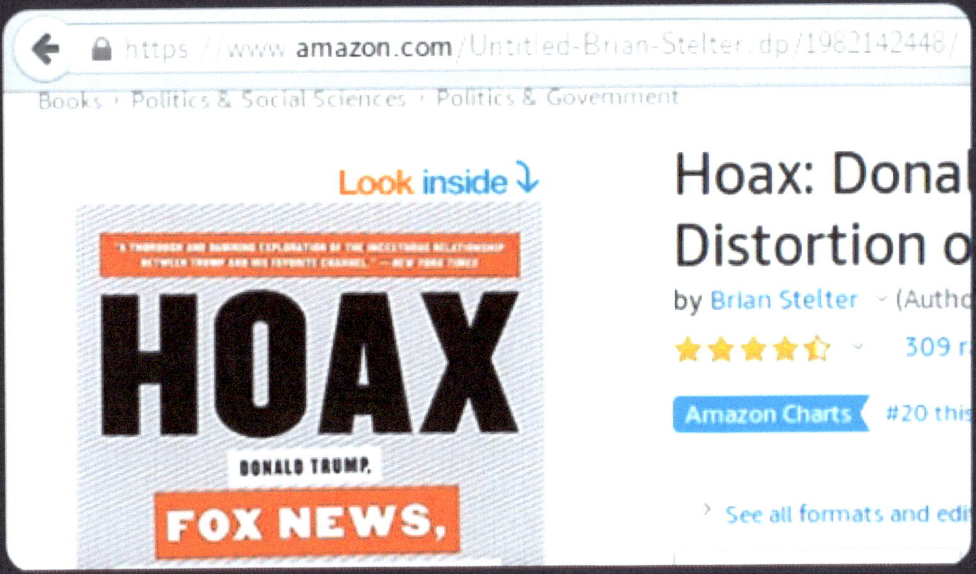

1

Communist Party of China @CommunistsChina · 15h

... MSNBC but quickly exited the Amazon bestseller list.

WHO'S FEELING GOOD ABOUT THE OVER-SENSITIVE CORONAVIRUS TEST KITS (RT-PCR)

Communist Party of China @CommunistsChina

When Western people try to return to work and get tested, Chairman say alarmist Western media spin increase in "positive" test cases as rapid increase in coronavirus infections. Stone Age tribes with minimal contact with outside world also test positive. All thanks to the non-standard "rapid" PCR test kit. In Africa, suspicious officials found even goat test positive with over-sensitive WHO test kit.

Business Standard

Diagnostics too sensitive: Your Covid test is positive. Should it be?

Apoorva Mandavilli | NYT | | August 30 2020

Some of the nation's leading public health experts are raising a new concern in the endless debate over coronavirus testing in the United States: The standard tests are diagnosing huge numbers of people who may be carrying relatively insignificant amounts of the virus.

All members of Great Andamanese tribe recover from COVID-19

Communist Party of China @CommunistsChina · 15h

@realDonaldTrump Trump Derangement Syndrome explained.

1. Trump says support the police. The Left says defund the police.
2. Trump says ready to debate Biden. The Left says scrap the debates. (NYT)
3. Trump promises vaccine. The Left says the ...

Foreign Policy

Trump's Coronavirus Vaccine Can't Be Trusted

Trump's Vaccine Can't Be Trusted ... Services Secretary Alex Azar stripped the FDA of authority to approve, or deny, licensing of COVID tests.

2 weeks ago

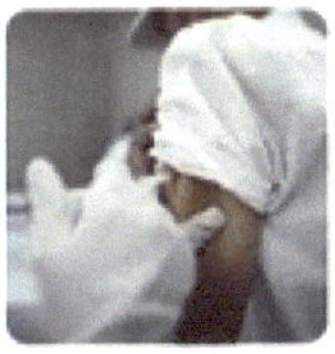

1

Communist Party of China
@CommunistsChina

Replying to @CommunistsChina

... vaccines cannot be trusted so soon.
4. Trump nominated for Nobel Prize. The Left says 'End the Nobel Peace Prize'. (The Atlantic)

Communist Party of China
@CommunistsChina

Chairman say man falling behind monkeys in evolutionary tree.

Baboons Prowl UK Safari Park "Carrying Knives & Chainsaws", Sparking Chaos

Workers are on edge *at a popular safari park after baboons were spotted wielding tools like* ***knives, screwdrivers, and even a chainsaw...***

Communist Party of China
@CommunistsChina

Chairman ask translation of "Stay control save. Alert virus lives."

Eleven Jinping has banned number Xi in China

Communist Party of China
@CommunistsChina

#ElonMusk's decision to change his kid's name from "X Æ A-12" to "X Æ A-Xii" has upset Xi... President Xi Jinpeng, my politburo sources tell me.

The number 11 is banned in the Chinese Internet.

Elon Musk And Grimes Change Their Newborn's Name From "X Æ A-12" To "X Æ A-Xii"

"First of all, my partner is the one that, actually, mostly, came up with the name. Yeah, she's great at names," Musk said. Sure, if you say so.

View Tweet activity

AOC - All Over Climate

Alexandria Ocasio-Cortez @AOC · Jul 5
US House candidate, NY-14
Yes, that is precisely why the party nominated... Joe Biden

> **Ted Cruz** @tedcruz · Jul 5
> Dems support the riots. The vandals. The anarchists.
>
> That's their base. And they're terrified to offend them.
> twitter.com/KimStrassel/st...

7.6K 17.1K 168.5K

Alexandria Ocasio-Cortez @AOC · Jul 5
US House candidate, NY-14
Is it me, or is the GOP losing their touch with the conspiracy-theory-as-campaign-rhetoric technique?

3.5K 6K 92K

Communist Party of China

@CommunistsChina

Replying to @AOC

It is you.

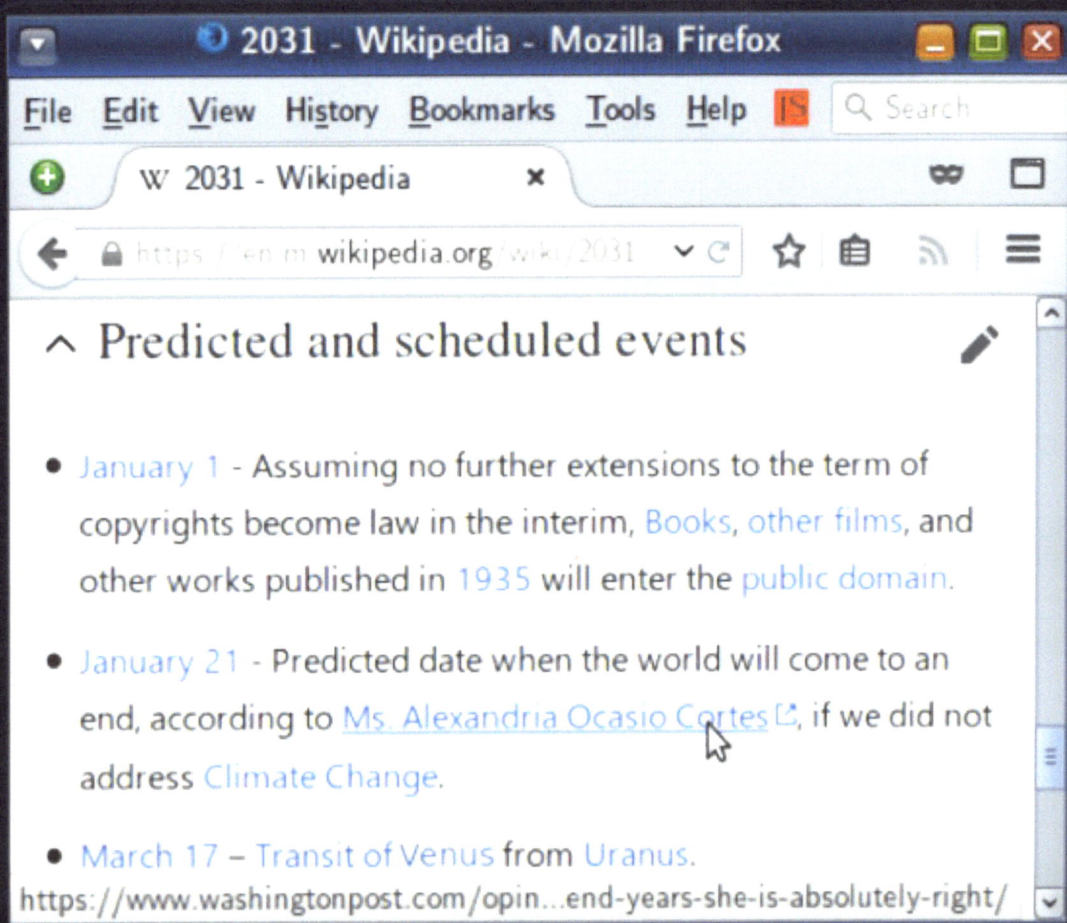

Global Cooling

Communist Party of China @CommunistsChina · 28m

Confucius ask if melted water have cooling effect?

#Warming #Hoax

Antarctica To Lift Seas By Metres Per Degree Of Warming, Study Finds

Freedom to spread propaganda

Communist Party of China @CommunistsChina

Western media publish story North Korean president Kim Jong-Un dead. President Kim call it horse excrement by showing up at fertilizer factory. Western media so full of horse excrement they fail to note any sarcasm!

"Ashy & Bloated": Analysts Pore Over Kim Jong Un Photos For Clues To Mystery Absence

Experts zero in on **fresh puncture mark seen on the leader's right wrist...**

Exception to the rule?

Communist Party of China
@CommunistsChina

The US stared down the mighty Soviet Union but chickened out before a Chinese mobile app. #sad

CFIUS Gives Microsoft 45 Days For TikTok Deal Talks As ByteDance Shifts HQ To London

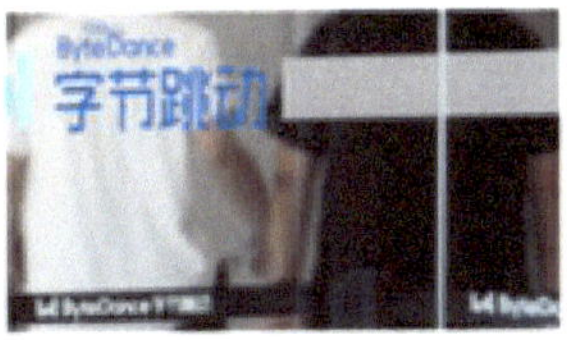

Will the White House and Beijing hammer out a compromise after all?

Central banks or printing presses?

Communist Party of China
@CommunistsChina

Imperialist Americans say their bubble bigger than all others.

The US Economy Is Stronger Than The Eurozone

*These figures **contradict the calls for a stronger Euro** vs the US Dollar...*

Deep State used to steal foreign elections with USAID funds

James O'Keefe @JamesOKeefeIII · 2h

The most viewed video in @Project_Veritas history #CashForBallots

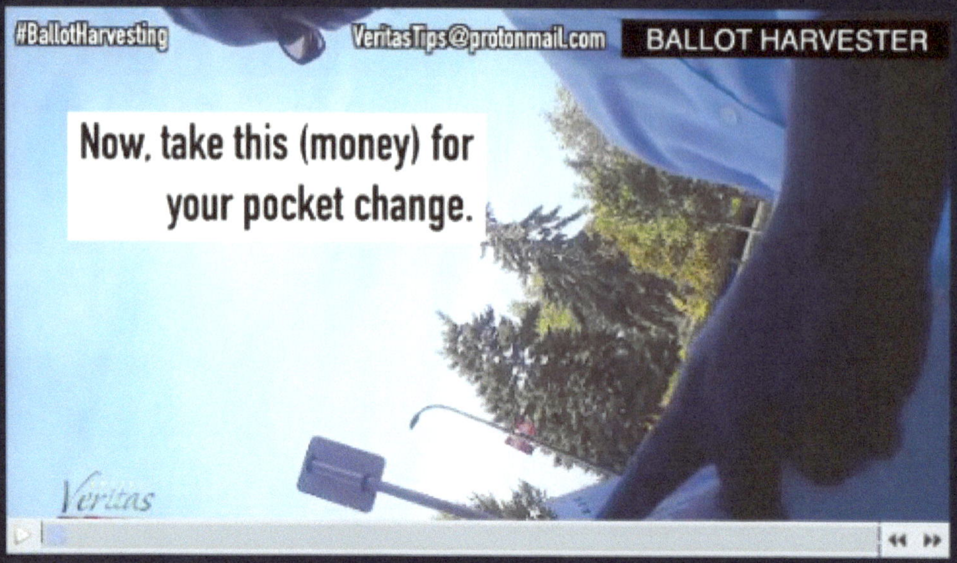

From **James O'Keefe**

Communist Party of China

@CommunistsChina

Replying to @JamesOKeefeIII

"Ah-ha," Chairman Mao exclaim, "the chicken come back home to roost!" After stealing elections abroad ("colour revolutions") with USAID money, George Soros is now stealing the American election.

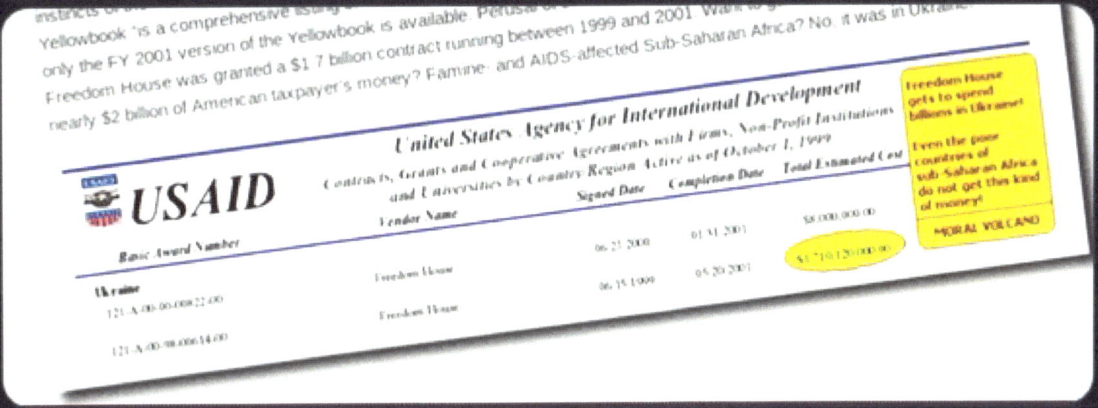

Communist Party of China
@CommunistsChina

Chairman ask. Is there any woman in America not yet raped by Weinstein, Epstein or Bill Clinton?

"No, not, Hillary!", Chairman clarify.

Weinstein's ex-assistant describes how he tried to rape her in new documentary

Is the Devil a Vatican employee?

Communist Party of China
@CommunistsChina

"Vatican's chief exorcist dealt with the Devil 60k times in 30 years"

Or an average of 2000 per year or 5.5 times per day.

The Devil must be a Vatican employee!

Head-spinning story of Vatican's chief exorcist for 30 years...

Dealt with devil 60,000 times...

Pinhead

Communist Party of China
@CommunistsChina

Confucius say man bad news if head smaller than neck.

Footballer serving 22-YEAR jail sentence over murder of model whose body was fed to DOGS faces tag dispute after joining new club

Nancy Pansy Pelosi

Mayor Bill de Blasio @NYCMayor · Jun 8

A lot has been happening this week, to say the least. And we're getting ready for a very big moment tomorrow as Phase One of the Re-Start begins. So I want to make life a little easier for all of us: Alternate Side Parking is cancelled tomorrow Mon June 8 thru Sun June 21.

Carlos Maza @gaywonk · Jun 8

Whose dick do I have to suck to get you to resign

Communist Party of China
@CommunistsChina

Replying to @gaywonk

Kneel before @SpeakerPelosi

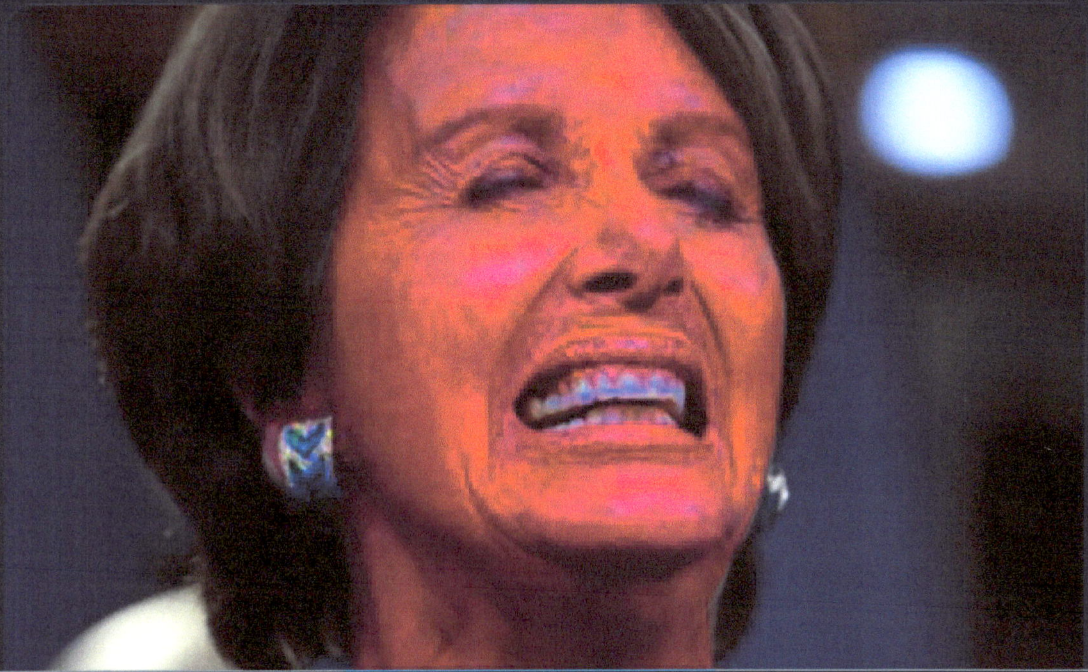

NEW SPEAK TIMES: BLACK IS WHITE & WHITE IS BLACK

New York Times Opinion @nytopinion · Sep 26

"Trump wants you to think Biden is senile, out of it," writes @nytegan. Yet "this is the president who confused 9/11 with 7-Eleven, who gave us covfefe, the nation of Thighland, and that great national park, Yo-Semite."

Opinion | Joe Biden's Stutter Is His Superpower
He already knows how to face down a bully.
nytimes.com

Communist Party of China @CommunistsChina · 29s

The Democratic presidential candidate Biden portrayed Black juvenile offenders as super-predators

https://www.youtube.com/watch?v=HXPZ2msLiU0

says JOBS is a three-letter word, claimed Blacks are not Blacks if they did not vote for him, and called for the arrest of deceased Black ...

People of Color, meet Politicians of Convenience

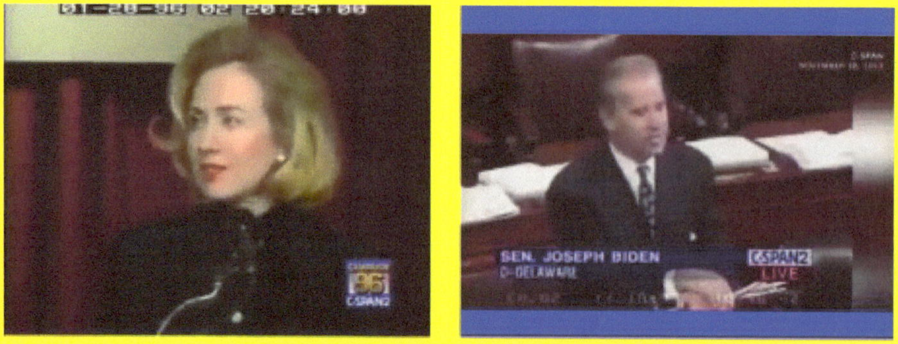

#PeopleOfColour vs. Politicians of Convenience (#Jo...
Source: C-Span
youtube.com

Communist Party of China
@CommunistsChina

Replying to @CommunistsChina

... victim Breonna Taylor. Of course, NYT is handicapped as well

New York Times' Mara Gay mocked for attacking 'racist Twitte...
New York Times editorial board member Mara Gay had some choice words for the "racist Twitter mob" who went after her
foxnews.com

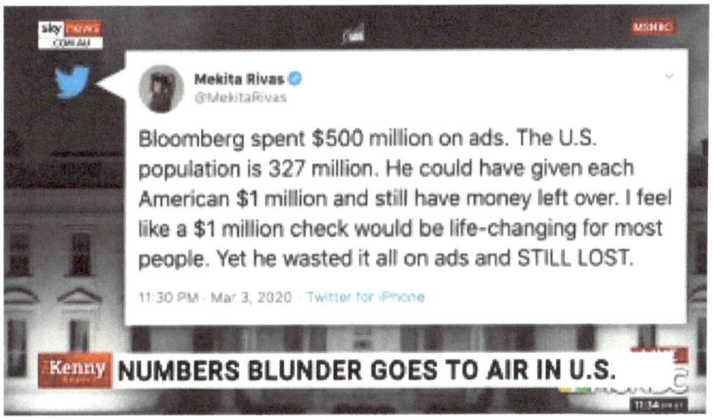

MSNBC host, New York Times journalist make huge on-air maths blunder

COMMUNIST DICKS LEAVE FEMINISTS DISSATISFIED

Communist Party of China
@CommunistsChina

Chairman Mao say People's Daily's new building prove Communists are not just hammer-and-sickle but real tools.

Chairman ask why Feminists blow their top off...

▲ Masculine monument ... the office building of the People's Daily newspaper, Beijing, which was mocked for its phallic appearance. Photograph: Imaginechina/Rex Features

Communist Party of China @CommunistsChina · 12m

Replying to @CommunistsChina

thecollegefix.com/feminist-geogr...

"Upward-thrusting buildings ejaculating light into the night sky"

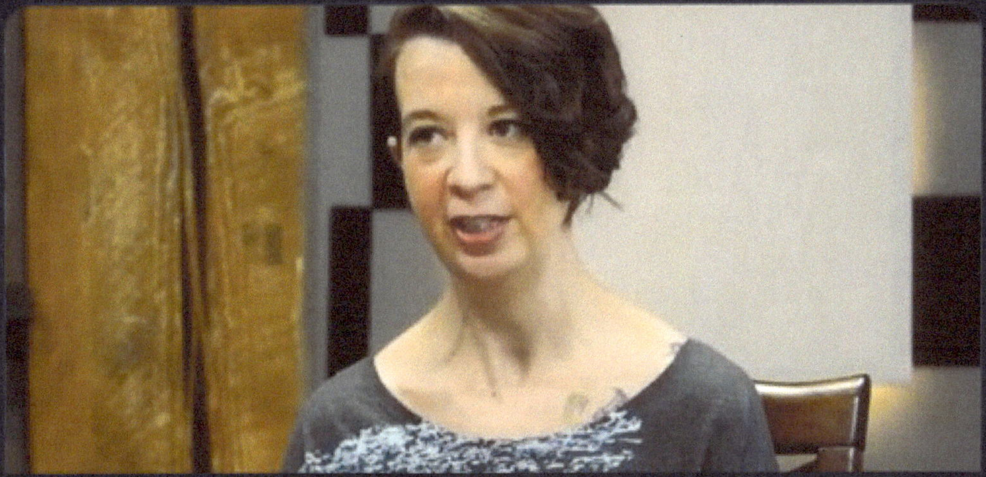

'Feminist geography' professor argues tall buildings are sexist | The Coll...

Upward-thrusting buildings ejaculating light into the night sky,' says Leslie Kern.

thecollegefix.com

Fact-check a joke and save humanity

PolitiFact @PolitiFact · 6h

The Trump campaign falsely claimed Biden promoted a white power symbol. Biden was signaling "zero" to illustrate his claims about corporations and Trump paying "zero" in taxes in the past. Pants on Fire!

> **Trump War Room - Text TRUMP to 88022** @TrumpWarRo... · 12h
>
> Last week Joe Biden flashed the "white power" sign.
>
> President Trump condemned white supremacists yesterday. Why hasn't Joe Biden?

Communist Party of China
@CommunistsChina

Replying to @PolitiFact

Chairman Mao thanks you for saving Leftist snowflakes from an obvious joke.

Sir, I'm going to have to ask you to leave the internet.
You're just too fucking stupid.
I'm from the Internet

Spy vs. Spy

Communist Party of China
@CommunistsChina

Chairman ask if American mobile phones and apps not steal data or track you? 🤑 🤓 😲 😨 😱

#MidlyAstonished

From the operating system level up, Western software are designed to act like spyware.

Xiaomi Could Be Sending Your Browser Data to China

Communist Party of China @CommunistsChina · 31m
Chairman say #Communists successfully infiltrate West.

FBI running WEEKLY struggle sessions on 'intersectionality' in the name of diversity and anti-racism – report

Books By Moral Volcano

Reptilian News Cartoons v2020

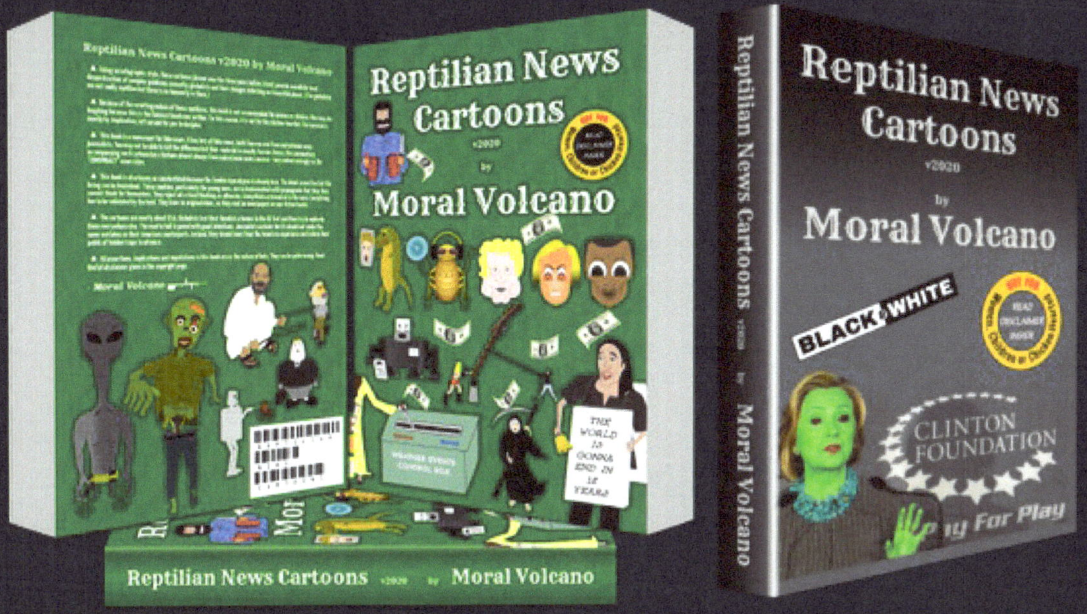

- Buy
    - Paperback (full color) - $60
    - Paperback (grayscale) - $11
    - Ebook - $3
- Description
    - Using an infographic style, these cartoons (drawn over the three years before 2020) provide soundbite-level **deconstruction of complex problems caused by globalists** and their stooges infesting our beautiful planet. (The globalists are not really reptilian but there is no humanity in them.)
    - Because of the revolting nature of these reptilians, this book is not recommended for women and children. However, men may die laughing. **This is the funniest book ever written.** The sarcasm is mostly by implication, left unsaid for you to decipher.
    - This book is a monument for fake news. It **has lots of fake news, both from me and from mainstream news journalists**. You may not be able to tell the difference but their material is usually funnier. Hence, the commentary accompanying each cartoon has citations almost always from mainstream news sources - very embarrassingly so. **No "CONSPIRACY" news sites.**
    - This book is also heavy on counterthink because the Zombie Apocalypse is already here. **The dead cannot live but the living can be braindead.** These zombies, particularly the young ones, are so brainwashed with propaganda that they they cannot think for themselves. They reject all critical thinking as offensive. Groupthink or hivemind is the norm. Everything has to be validated by the herd.

They have no original ideas, as they read no newspapers or non-fiction books.
  - The cartoons are mostly about USA. Globalists test their fiendish schemes in the US first and then try to replicate them everywhere else. The road to hell is paved with good intentions. **Journalists outside the US should not make the same mistakes as their American counterparts.** Instead, they should learn from the American experience and inform their public of hidden traps in advance.
  - All assertions, implications and imputations in this book are in the nature of bets. They can be quite wrong. **Read the full disclaimer given in the copyright page.**
  - This 30-MB full-color print-replica Kindle ebook contains 149 cartoons and commentary spread over 434 pages. It is also available in full-color paperback ($60) and black-n-white paperback ($11). A **free 70-page sample PDF with 12 cartoons is available** on the Moral Volcano blog: https://moralvolcano.wordpress.com/2020/02/29/the-reptilian-news-cartoons-book/
- Praise
  - Hillary Clinton
    "This is pure Indian propaganda!"
  - New York Times
    "This book is full of lies, mostly sourced from our newspaper and other mainstream media sources."
  - CNN
    "This book may have more fake news than CNN but it is not the quantity that matters."

Humorous Tweets By Chairman Mao v2021

- Price:
  - Paperback (full color) - $10.90
  - Ebook - $0

www.ingramcontent.com/pod-product-compliance
Ingram Content Group UK Ltd.
Pitfield, Milton Keynes, MK11 3LW, UK
UKHW061433190726
13845UKWH00021B/170
9789354199028